HASTINGS
IN OLD PHOTOGRAPHS

A favourite photographer's view of St Clement's Church; the camera on its tripod was still a novelty for arresting the attention, even of the small boys on the church wall.

HASTINGS
IN OLD PHOTOGRAPHS

COLLECTED BY
PAMELA HAINES

ALAN SUTTON

Alan Sutton Publishing
Phoenix Mill · Far Thrupp · Stroud · Gloucestershire

First published 1989

Reprinted 1993

British Library Cataloguing in Publication Data

Hastings in old photographs.
1. East Sussex. Hastings, history
1. Haines, Pamela
942.2′59

ISBN 0-86299-621-X

Dedicated to
David Vivian Haines
with love.

Typesetting and origination by
Alan Sutton Publishing.
Printed in Great Britain by
The Bath Press, Avon.

CONTENTS

INTRODUCTION

This selection of photographs dates from the mid-1850s to 1940. Photography arrived in Hastings in the 1850s, and the first-known picture of the sea front (included in this book) was taken in around 1857. A brief survey of the town will help you to understand the photographs and their meaning.

Although Hastings is now all one town, it consisted of three separate localities in the 1850s. The original Hastings – the Old Town, as it is still called – still survives with its own unique identity. Situated in the Bourne Valley, it started to grow into the adjacent Priory Valley at a much earlier date. However, it was in the early 1850s that this second and 'new' part of Hastings – sometimes known as Central Hastings – was extensively developed. The developer was a rather mysterious gentleman named Patrick Francis Robertson. All that is known of him is that he made his fortune in China and had a short spell as a Hastings MP. From photographs, however, we can be certain that his grand terraces were intended to rival the third locality known as St Leonards-on-Sea. This was actually a separate town, a mile to the west of Hastings. Building had begun there in 1828, and the intention of its architect and founder, James Burton, was the creation of an elegantly planned town for posterity. It was officially incorporated into its rival, Hastings, in 1888. (The outlying villages of Hollington and Ore followed in 1897.) This then, was the setting for the first photographers, giving their photographs their separate period flavours.

By 1865, one H.J. Godbold had appeared on the scene. Little is known of him, other than his address (No. 8 Grand Parade), and the strange fact that his real name was Godbolt. However, we do know from his pictures that he was one of several who deserved the growing prestige and authority of the 'artistic' photographers. Although he probably made much of his living from cartes-de-visites (portraits the size of visiting-cards), he was among the first to have the professional confidence to take large groups and public scenes. Many a photographer of those days (and even much later) could cope with small groups, but then, as now, children and small dogs often refused to stand still. Old ladies, too, could be very fidgity. Given the slow emulsions and shutter speeds of his time, a photographer like Godbold had to know how to make everyone keep still. This was more the outcome of having a commanding but tactful personality, we can be sure, than a mere ability to cry 'Watch the birdie'! At the same time, he would have needed dexterity in setting up the camera and handling it and outstanding technical ability in the darkroom.

Obviously, these qualities varied in the photographers and we can see the results in their work. Some, for example, chose to dodge the problem of moving figures by taking their photographs in the early morning. To some extent, this gives the location an unreal air, for then, as now, it is people who give reality to photographs. There is, however, no denying that an 'empty' location can have a special charm.

It was in the mid-1870s that Frederick Stephen Mann (of No. 13 Wellington Place) began to work his photographic way around Central Hastings. A member of a local family, he described himself as a 'photographic artist, carver and gilder'. It is from his now faded photographs that we find the eloquent testimony to Robertson's impressive plans.

The photographer J.W. Thomas of George Street is remembered today for his excellent portraits – mostly as cartes-de-visites, but included in this book is also his fine portrait study of Dr Elizabeth Blackwell. It was taken on whole-plate in her own home and is worth studying for the sheer clarity of the detail. Another photographer, J.H. Blomfield of Robertson Street, was at pains to describe himself not just as a photographic artist, but as a painter of portraits and miniatures.

Another photographer who came to live in Hastings was George Woods. He became so familiar a figure in the 1890s that people enjoyed posing for him. His artistic survey of the town has been published separately and his work, therefore, is not included in this book; he has to be mentioned, however, as his work is important to the study of photography in Hastings of that period. (His original plates are the property of the Hastings Museum and Hastings Reference Library.)

Following upon these pioneers, Fred Judge arrived in the early 1900s and set up his now famous postcard business. (It is still flourishing.) Judge concentrated on high quality work and by 1939 had produced 30,000 cards. He was a world-famous photographer in his own right and died in 1950. His postcards have been published elsewhere, but included in this book is a crowd scene showing the proclamation of King George V in 1910.

Another excellent photographer was working in Hastings in the early 1900s and deserves, in my opinion, to be better known. He was F.N. Broderick from Ryde, Isle of Wight. His postcards capture town life perfectly. You can always be sure that it is people who first catch Broderick's eye: holiday-makers; ladies out shopping; elderly gentlemen taking their quiet strolls along the promenade. Details of his life are scanty and some of his named work might have been done by his assistants, but all old photographs of this quality bear out the belief (then very controversial) that photography was an art.

The Edwardian period was the hey-day of the seaside postcard – showing all the bustling atmosphere of a holiday by the sea. Today, in Hastings, that atmosphere has been lost. Shingle has piled up and the old picturesque groynes have been replaced with concrete. Commercial amusements are now wedged in between the Old Town and the Fishing Beach – The Stade – and both beach and sea is under constant threat of pollution. The old-fashioned entertainments have gone: no Pierrots, minstrels or Punch-and-Judy are to be found on the beach of today. We only need to look at the pictures of the old pleasure yachts to see how much the romance and excitement of the seaside holiday has waned.

Modern progress is, however, not entirely to blame. By the early 1900s, Hastings was already a town which had begun to stand still. The rot had set in and much of the romance was a façade. The Victorian building boom was over and there was dire poverty and unemployment. This portentous atmosphere was brilliantly depicted by the Hastings writer, Robert Tressell, in his world-famous novel *The Ragged Trousered Philanthropists*. Published in 1914, the book is confirmed by old newspaper photographs of poor children, workhouse occupants and undernourished labourers. These pictures do not copy well in book form, but I have included a few samples of what can be found. The *Daily Mirror* was the first national daily paper to publish photographs (in 1904), and, in 1905, the local owner of the *Hastings Observer* (F.J. Parsons) began to use pictures in his other paper the *Hastings and St Leonards Advertiser*. The photographers are unknown and the original prints unobtainable. They were the first 'socially aware' pictures of Hastings.

Local commercial photographers found a living by working the beaches in summer, and, perhaps out of season, by taking the pictures of the proud owners of shops (and even their delivery-carts). With the outbreak of the First World War, they became just as busy in taking photographs of soldiers, their wives and sweethearts. The town was always full because the troops *en route* to the Channel Ports were billeted with local families. The rumble of the guns in France were distinctly heard in Hastings and soon the papers were full of pictures of war casualties.

After the First World War, the Town Council set about trying to up-grade the town as a seaside resort. From as early as 1908, public works had been photographed by the Borough Engineer's Department, and this practice continues today. So we do have a record from those earlier days of the civic efforts to remedy the situation. The inter-war years were certainly very active years of improvement. That particular period saw the reconstruction of the sea front, the remodelling of the White Rock Baths and the building of a new open-air bathing pool at West Marina. There were many other improvements. However, looking at the photographs and postcards of the time, we find a loss of charm. There is not the same atmosphere of exuberant humanity of the earlier periods. With a few exceptions, people often look very solemn – and we all know the reason. The onset of the Second World War was about to mark the end of an era. It certainly marked the end of romantic Hastings – a merely local era.

This brief history of photography in Hastings poses a final question. What is the value in studying old photographs? As an aspect of local history research, photographs arouse a lot of nostalgia for what seems to have been a more leisured and gracious way of life. More creatively, they can be used for reconstructing the background to family history. Students can study the history of architecture, trade, transport, costume and a lot more besides with the aid of old photographs. For the rest of us, even a most cursory glance at old photographs reveals the ugliness of modern reality. Present day shop signs, for example, are hideous when compared with earlier ones. Old photographs, as a study, can help to stop this sort of thing. They teach us to value what is fine in our heritage and stimulate us to protect it.

The Victorians

THE ALBERT MEMORIAL CLOCK TOWER (built 1862) was damaged by fire and pulled down in 1973. It is still mourned by the natives. Taken from the bottom of Cambridge Road, this scene is still recognizable as the heart of Victorian Hastings. However, the truly magnificent gas-lamp has gone.

HASTINGS AND THE RAILWAY STATION.

THE FIRST ILLUSTRATION of Hastings Railway Station (1851) shortly before photography of the town began. Use a magnifying glass to discern the six coaches emerging from the tunnel. The Victorian town centre is just being built in the curve of the cliff (on the left) by the sea. To the right of the three gossiping locals is Wellington Square, built 30 years earlier and still impressive today. (Illustrated London News.)

THE EARLIEST KNOWN PHOTOGRAPH of Hastings sea front (1857). But here is a puzzle. Where was it taken from? Not the pier, as many might imagine. The pier was not then built. So how did the photographer achieve the angle? From the deck of a beached boat? From up a ladder? Nobody knows. (The white objects in the left-hand corner are washing laid flat to dry on the shingle.)

A FADED PICTURE from the 1880s of White Rock with some bath chair men waiting for customers. The large building with three arches is Rock & Co., a flourishing firm of carriage builders (now Courts the furnishers). A magnifying glass will reveal the porticoed premises (six buildings further up) of the White Rock Brewery. Next to it is the half-built Palace Hotel (now Palace Chambers).

NOTE THE GOAT. Seats like this are still in position, but now have no clear view of the sea as the underground car-park is now immediately in front of them. (Broderick.)

THE FOLLOWING SIX PHOTOGRAPHS by F.S. Mann (mid-1870) can be used on a brief but fascinating 'then and now walk'. This is the town centre end of Robertson Street taken from the direction of the memorial clock tower (now a traffic island). The ghostly figures are the pedestrians who were walking too quickly to be captured by the slow shutter speed.

ROBERTSON STREET, looking eastwards from the corner of Claremont. Taken 20 years after the street was built, this photograph shows the gradual conversion of a residential terrace into a line of shops. The conversion was far more 'sympathetic' than we find today. An enticing example is the first shop to the right – Madame Leapman's Old Curiosity Shop.

ROBERTSON STREET. The building to the left (square tower) was the first Robertson Street Congregational Church. Rebuilt and enlarged in 1885, it is now the United Reformed Church. The houses to the right of the church are shortly to be demolished for the town centre relief road.

CLAREMONT, taken from the western end of Robertson Street and the basis of the so-called Trinity triangle i.e., the three roads enclosing Holy Trinity Church. Known to generations of public library borrowers and art students using 'the Brassey', Claremont always had an atmosphere of its own with its unusual and rather exclusive shops. Today, alas, the atmosphere has almost evaporated, but vestiges remain. Originally built as lodging houses, only the buildings Nos. 10 and 11 have their original wrought iron balconies.

BACK AT THE TOWN CENTRE. This view of Havelock Road was taken from the direction of the Memorial clock tower. Named after General Havelock, a Victorian hero of the Indian Mutiny, this road leads to the railway station and was built soon after the station opened in 1852. It is actually an artificial hill, consisting of spoil from the railway tunnel.

CAMBRIDGE ROAD AGAIN, but further down and taken from the position of the supermarket. The two terraced houses on the right are soon to vanish to facilitate the town centre relief road.

CAMBRIDGE ROAD, mid-1870s. The houses on the left centre were replaced in the 1930s by a cinema and later by a supermarket. Further down, the terrace of houses with blinds drawn down is now the site of the central post office.

ENGRAVINGS were being used with photographs until the end of the nineteenth century, to illustrate guide books. This shows the coastguard's at St Michaels, White Rock. Behind him is the new town centre looking east towards Wellington Square and the castle. To the left on the skyline are the last two windmills on the West Hill. Taken in around 1860.

A VICTORIAN LION AND A UNICORN stand at each end of Robertson Terrace and are said to have been acquired from Buckingham Palace. Nobody knows the full story. They have weathered well, but today have to gaze majestically out to sea over the roar of sea-front traffic. Mr P.F. Robertson must have been quite a character to have acquired these royal animals.

A RUSSIAN GUN was brought to Hastings in 1857, as a tribute to the men who had fought in the Crimea. Near Pelham Crescent.

THIS CORNER IN ROBERTSON STREET (1880) has not changed much. The memorial fountain to the Countess Waldegrave is more dilapidated, but there are still shops on the right-hand side, with awnings but without the stanchions. Behind the fountain, you can see the east end of Holy Trinity church. Started in 1857, it took a long time to build, because the first vicar, Dr Crosse, refused (as he put it) to beg for money from his parishioners. The view gives no indication of the beauty of the interior – one of the finest in Hastings. Look down the road on the right. The building in Venetian-Gothic style is still known as 'the Brassey', i.e. the Brassey Institute, built in 1878 by Lord Brassey and given by him for use as today's public library.

THE TOWN CENTRE OF HASTINGS in the early 1900s, complete with a wet surface of dust and horse dung. The motor bus on the extreme left heralds a new age with its bold advertisement for electric lighting. This came to Hastings in 1882, but it was to be many years before gas was ousted completely.

HASTINGS has never been a good beach for shell collecting, as the shingle breaks up any shells. So these two ladies are selling exotic but imported shells. Visitors were probably allowed to think they came from nearby waters and were brought in by the fishermen. This is a remarkably deserted picture of a sea front area which was usually very busy. A large part of the castle cliff (behind) and some of the castle itself was cut away to build the beautiful Regency-style terrace (1828). The shops in front of it were designed as an arcade and had unique wine vaults beneath them.

EAST PARADE, with the mini-spire of the lifeboat house in the distance. Opened in 1882, this attractive Victorian building was pulled down in 1959. The sea front has been considerably widened at this point, but you can still see the houses on the left opposite the boating lake.

ORE VILLAGE in the 1880s. Faintly, on the skyline, right of centre, is the White Mill. Extreme right: a poster advertising the London, Brighton and South Coast Railway. Christ Church, on the left, is a Victorian church, interesting mainly because it now possesses some chancel murals painted in the early 1900s thought to be by Robert Tressell.

HASTINGS HOUSE, where the Duke of Wellington spent his honeymoon in 1806 and where the poet Byron threw ink over the statue (just left of the door). The house was demolished to make way for Old Humphrey Avenue. Behind are the home-made antiquities known as the 'Black Arches', created by enterprising locals to please ignorant visitors.

THIS PICTURE OF ALL SAINTS CHURCH in 1870 is of particular interest for its view (now almost faded) of the West Hill, with only part of Priory Road having been built.

THE LAST REMAINING WINDMILL on the West Hill. This one stood at the beginning of Priory Road and was pulled down in 1874.

THE WEST HILL in the 1900s showing the widened Priory Road and the houses built on the site of the windmill.

ROCK-A-NORE ROAD in the 1890s. On the left at East Cliff House is Edward Smith's furniture store. The two pubs to the right are the Prince Albert Tavern and The Star in the East.

MOVING HOUSE in the early 1900s would have meant employing Tapner & Woodman of Waterworks Road. Horse-drawn pantechnicons were in use for many years.

MEADOW COTTAGES, Meadow Road. Named after the Priory Meadow (the cricket ground), Meadow Road became Queen's Road in 1876 out of loyalty to Her Majesty. These 1819 cottages, now demolished, were on the site of Ward's, the present-day outfitters. This is a good example of local vernacular weather-board building which is still to be seen in the Old Town.

VICTORIAN PHOTOGRAPHERS often found it difficult to take street scenes because pedestrians and bystanders would move and blur the print. This is why so many street scenes are taken in the very early morning. This 1880s photographer skilfully posed a few people outside the South Colonnade shops (to the right). Dorman's Library and Reading Room produced guide books to St Leonards in the 1860s and '70s.

THE ROYAL VICTORIA HOTEL, built by James Burton in 1828/9. This view, almost certainly taken by the famous photographer Frances Frith, in 1864, shows the hotel before it was enlarged in the 1890s. The entrance was then at the back so that visitors could arrive well-sheltered from the sea front weather. With the Assembly Rooms behind, it became the social centre of St Leonards and attracted the famous and wealthy. The Hotel has recently been redecorated attractively in the style of the period in which it was built. Opposite are some striped bathing-huts. You can see that the ladders, used to step into the sea, are folded underneath.

THIS ALMOST DESERTED SCENE of around 1880, shows the East Lodge Gate – the boundary entrance to Burton's St Leonards – and the St Leonard's Parade opposite the sea. The Parade was usually thronged with fashionable people and was a paradise for royalty watchers. Foreign royal families and nobility flocked to St Leonards. Hastings people were at first very stand-offish about this new town on their doorstep; the potential for making money out of it was then swiftly appreciated and hawkers from Hastings were soon annoying the St Leonards shopkeepers. The South Colonnade, behind the two figures on the left, is the line of elegantly designed shops provided for St Leonards. There is a grocer's at this near end. A gap in the railings (to the right of the two figures) gives access to a boot and shoe shop in the south part of the arch.

MUCH HISTORICAL CONFUSION attaches itself to the family who owned this enormous mansion at Catsfield, near Hastings. It took five years to build and was completed in 1870. The man who paid for it all was the famous and fabulously wealthy Thomas Brassey, the railway contractor. He gave it to his son, the Thomas Brassey who became MP for Hastings in 1868 and, later, the Earl Brassey. The identities of father, son and grandson are the sources of confusion, to say nothing of the confusion over Earl Brassey's two wives. The Brassey family liked to think they had Norman blood, hence the name of the house, Normanhurst, and the attempt to site this Victorian French chateau as near to the site of the Battle of Hastings as possible. It was a great tourist attraction in its day. The entrance fees went to medical charities, but, eventually, the fee had to be raised to one shilling 'to encourage a better class of visitor'. The house was demolished in 1951 after being used by the army during the Second World War. A well-run caravan site now occupies the estate, but parts of the old terrace have remained.

THE FIRST KNOWN PHOTOGRAPH of Hastings Town Council. They had been invited to visit Normanhurst by the owner, Thomas Brassey, MP for Hastings. Brassey stands to the right of the door and is hatless. Date 1870.

COGHURST HALL in the 1870s. The beautiful coach is called a 'gentleman's private drag' and is complete with liveried servants. The coat of arms on the door denotes ownership by the Brisco family. Their mansion behind, rebuilt by Decimus Burton for Musgrave Brisco in 1834, replaced an earlier house. It was built of White Stone which gives a 'stately' effect. The reason for this photograph is not known, but perhaps it was a new coach' It comes from an album owned by the Brassey family who often employed top London photographers. We ourselves can picture the photographer setting up in the shade of the tree while the coachman has eyeball to eyeball control over the leading horse.

HALTON HOUSE. This mysterious photograph by an unknown photographer is intriguing because the house, which no longer exists, was the 1850 residence of Patrick Francis Robertson, MP. Although he was an MP for Hastings and the developer of the Robertson Street area, little is known of him. The house was built in 1824 for the Revd George Stonestreet, who served as a chaplain at the Battle of Waterloo. It stood in six acres of beautifully wooded grounds in Halton, on the western slopes above Hastings Old Town. The architecture is similar in style to the work of James and Decimus Burton.

THIS SERENE LOOKING OLD LADY is Dr Elizabeth Blackwell (1821–1910) at her home at Rock House, Exmouth Place, in May 1906. She was of English birth, but was the first woman doctor to gain medical qualifications in the USA. She wrote several books in Hastings upon moral health and frequently wrote letters to the local press. A quotation from her 'What can be done for the protection of our picturesque and protective East Hill? Surely the depredations of speculators ought to be stopped by our town councillors?' (J.W. Thomas.)

THIS VICTORIAN WORTHY with the Shakespearian brow is Thomas Brandon Brett (1816–1906). A man of tremendous energy, he rose from errand boy to editor and publisher of his own newspaper (known as *Brett's Gazette*). His many interests included music and education. He also wrote excruciatingly bad verse. Brett's voluminous works include much local history detail (now on micro-film) which can be studied in Hastings Reference Library.

THE SOCIETY OF ST LEONARDS ARCHERS was founded in 1833 in a hollow (possibly a disused quarry), which is now the site of the Hastings College of Further Education. This photograph dates from 1865 when the society held its most successful meeting. Five hundred spectators watched 43 archers competing. This shows the prize giving. (H.J. Godbold.)

INTEREST IN ARCHERY HAD DECLINED by 1880. The society was, however, revived between 1894 and 1932. Victorian ladies found they enjoyed archery. It was one of the few sports where they could compete with men and also enjoy their company. The prizes and trophies are now in the Hastings Museum. This photograph dates from the late 1890s.

NOMINATION DAY, 1865. This faded and damp-spotted picture is the very first photograph of an election in Hastings. It shows the open air booth, known as the hustings, on what is now the cricket ground – this being the Conservative hustings. The faintly discernible buildings behind the hustings are railway sheds.

NOMINATION DAY, 1865, this time showing the Liberal hustings in another part of the cricket ground. Their proximity accounts for the fact that elections were rough, noisy and boisterous. However, in spite of the rowdiness, there are plenty of ladies present. (Later, Hastings became a hot bed of suffragette agitation.) The two MPs elected were The Hon. G. Waldegrave-Leslie (Liberal) and P.F. Robertson (Conservative). This and the previous photograph were taken by H.J. Godbold.

A RARE PHOTOGRAPH of the ex-Liberal Prime Minister W.E. Gladstone leaving Hastings Station after lunching in the second class refreshment room. (It was especially decorated for the occasion and this was one of two triumphal arches.) The 82 year-old was in fine form and spoke for one and a half hours at the Gaiety Theatre (now a cinema) in Queen's Road. His drive back to the station was enlivened by a drunken postillion who knocked down some of the greenery from one of the arches. The postillion, Charles Davis, was arrested at the station and later fined £1 7s. 6d. Gladstone is behind the left horse, but someone (a political opponent?) seems to have scratched the surface of the photograph. Unknown photographer. Date: 17 March 1891.

HARRY GEORGE LONG, newsagent, at the door of his shop, No. 88 Norman Road, St Leonards, in the 1890s. William, his father, was a veteran of the Crimean War and a local temperance evangelist who had opened a confectioner's at No. 90 Norman Road in 1880. Harry Long died in 1897, but the business was continued by his daughter Edith Long a few doors away (at No. 72) until her death in 1974.

WAITING FOR THE CHRISTMAS TRADE. William Mercer with his sisters Nellie and Edith. This is Abergeldie Stores on the corner of Sedlescombe Road North and Duke Road. The windows are full of Christmas fare with rabbits dangling from the pole. The shop was built in the garden of Abergeldie House in 1894.

FASHIONABLE LADIES in the ruins of Hastings Castle in the 1860s. Crinolines were very dangerous in a high wind and the wearers could spin around like tops. This must have been a very calm day.

ST CLEMENT'S CAVES, 1880. Photography was impracticable in these spooky caverns. (This is an oil lithograph.) Visits by candlelight were a thrilling experience. The large statue on the left had several names which depended upon the favourite bogey-man as fancied by the guides.

THIS AND THE FOLLOWING THREE PHOTOGRAPHS are very heavily 'retouched' examples of guide book illustration. Here, a wagonette is off on a trip to Fairlight Glen via the cliff top lanes.

THE LADY on the left wears a boater hat, obviously anchored with a formidable hat-pin. She wears the striped blouse with wide sleeves which were very fashionable in the 1890s.

THE BATHING HUT STEPS provided shady seats.

ALTHOUGH MEN AND BOYS bathed nude earlier in the nineteenth century, nude bathing was prohibited in the 1890s. We do not know if these young men are getting into bathing-drawers before entering the water or are about to divest themselves of their last male undergarment.

A TYPICAL BEACH PHOTOGRAPHER IN ACTION. He has just got a group together, but, before getting under his black cloth, he is waiting for the inclusion of some obviously reluctant children.

PADDLING was always popular, and the sleepy-looking boatman seems not to have any customers. They appear to be ignoring him rather pointedly.

TWO CONTRASTING PHOTOGRAPHS of the sea front in the 1890s. This one was taken from the upstairs window of a house in Carlisle Parade.

FROM THE CORNER OF CARLISLE PARADE, this shows the two sets of steps which lead down to the old White Rock swimming baths. The baths nearest the camera were intended as an aquarium, but money ran out and it became a small bath for ladies.

THIS BEAUTIFUL PANORAMIC VIEW of the low water sands stretches westwards towards Hastings Pier in the 1880s. The ladies are still clinging to the constraints of the bustle, although the children are happily dressed for summer.

JOHNNY HUNTER, Entertainments Manager, Hastings Pier. After starting as a singer of comic songs, he was appointed manager in 1879 for the then amazing sum of £20 per week. Although he made the pier an enormous financial success, he resigned in 1909 after a dispute with his directors.

CHARLES HAWKER, the more elegant of the two, was Assistant Manager to Johnny Hunter. They were a highly successful team, despite their different characters. The pier was the only place of local entertainment open all the year.

ON A BANK HOLIDAY, some 30,000 people paid to go through these turnstiles, but the photographer has chosen to present the pier as devoid of all life. The poster on the left advertises paddle steamer trips to Brighton and Eastbourne. Other posters reveal what a lively amenity the Pier must have been.

AN ENTRANCE TO THE PIER PAVILION with a fire-engine on the left and a castellated ticket box (for the steamers) on the right.

THE WEST SIDE OF HASTINGS PIER in the 1880s, showing the intricate ironwork of the 'Eastern-style Pavilion'.

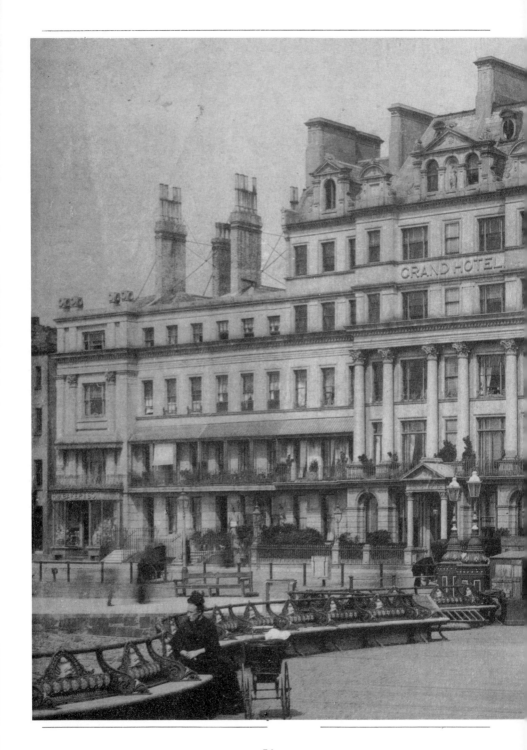

THIS SUPERB PHOTOGRAPH perhaps gives a clue to the identity of the photographer. To the right Messrs Boning and Small, art photographers, with a striped canvas awning are very noticeable. The Grand Hotel was built in 1882 as the Verulam Hotel, but changed its name soon after. It was originally known as 'Rascal's Row', but the reason for this (unfortunately for us) is now not known. The intricate ironwork of the pier was made by Messrs Laidlaw of Glasgow and was shipped to Hastings. Verulam Place has been rebuilt as Waverly Court in 1989.

TO THE ANNOYANCE of the Hastings Pier Co., this new pier was built at St Leonards in 1891. It became the first home of the Municipal Orchestra. A town councillor (obviously a resident of St Leonards) declared that St Leonards people were 'more receptive' to music than the people of Hastings. A superior feature of this pier was the additional pavilion at the entrance, so that carriages could drive to the door.

THIS SOLID BRICK AND TILE VICTORIAN SUMMER-HOUSE was built against the west curtain wall of Hastings Castle. We include the picture lest any future archaeologists should be baffled by traces of this long demolished building. (A previous excavation in the castle ruins revealed its Victorian flower-bed and caused confusion.)

ECCLESBOURNE GLEN (now part of the Country Park). This shows the coastguard cottages on the right. Threatened by coastal erosion, the last remains were demolished in 1961. Surviving coastguard cottages (now private houses) can be seen today further along the cliffs at Fairlight. Opposite to the top left of this picture you can see the targets of the firing range.

ANOTHER INTRIGUING PICTURE: Lover's Seat, Fairlight Glen in around 1890. Children were adept at making money from visitors to this romantic beauty spot overlooking the sea. This little girl, in a spotless pinafore and doubtless her mother's hat, is selling lemonade. Her equipment includes a three-legged bamboo table and a covered cooling-basket. The two ladies are in deepest mourning, in the hot weather these were scarcely the right clothes for the long trudge from the nearest road.

ALEXANDRA PARK, the Boating Lake. The lady on the path wears the more relaxed costume of the turn of the century, a comfortable blouse and skirt with a stylish boater hat. She carries an umbrella to shield her complexion from the sun, but has probably taken it down at the behest of the photographer who posed her. Today, this vantage point has a virtually identical skyline but the boats are made of plastic.

THE STOLIDLY WATCHFUL PARKKEEPER is in Gensing Gardens, St Leonards, a favourite playground for children. This sheltered and warm spot for subtropical plants and shrubs needed vigilant protection. Behind is Anglesea Terrace (still surviving) built at the same time as the laying out of the gardens in around 1880.

THIS UNIQUE TRIUMPHAL ARCH was raised by the fishermen of Hastings to welcome Lord Brassey when he returned to Sussex in 1900. (He had been away for five years as Governor of Victoria, Australia.) It was constructed from fishing nets, lobster pots, lifebelts, buoys, anchors, fishing barrels and coloured ships' lanterns. On top, you can see a dinghy. Flags bedecked the arch and the length of the street. (Mr Overton.)

WHITE ROCK in 1899. These are volunteers *en route* to enlist at Shorncliffe for the South African War. Of the 400 volunteers, only half were mounted and (complete with their bedding-rolls) are behind an artillery officer in the lead with a bugler behind him.

WARRIOR SQUARE STATION, date unknown. The inscription tells us that Mr Charles Arthur Kennett is standing beside Mr Bishop Kennett, the station master appointed in 1877. Both appear to be going off for a day's shooting with their dogs. The two dog kennels are a homely touch of the kind not seen, alas, on railway stations today.

A LATER PHOTOGRAPH of unknown date of the staff of Warrior Square Station. Back row, second left, Mr Alfred Ernest Kennett. Front row, second right (wearing a more sporty cap and off-hand attitude), Mr Bishop Kennett Junior. (J. Birchall, No. 32 Cambridge Road.)

A FORECOURT VIEW of Warrior Square Station (formerly Gensing Station) when it still belonged to the South Eastern and Chatham Railway Company.

THIS MAGNIFICENT VIADUCT was built in 1901 to connect Bexhill to the Hastings–Charing Cross line. It was blown up in 1968 as it had become redundant. The picture shows flooding of the marshes – not a river.

NAVVIES on the Sidley–Crowhurst line which was begun in 1897.

NGS STATION-DEPARTURE PLATFORM.
SOUTH EASTERN & CHATHAM RY.

IT IS EASY TO MISTAKE this postcard (published by McCorquodale & Co. in 1910) for a photograph. It is a water-colour used for an official railway poster. Although accurate in detail, the three locomotives (one is on the extreme right) are an unlikely combination on these platforms. The station was used by two rival companies: The London, Brighton and South Coast Railway, and the South Eastern and Chatham Railway. The SE line (on the left) went to Charing Cross via Ashford and Tunbridge Wells; the LBSC line (on the right) was the terminus of trains to Brighton and Victoria. The station was entirely rebuilt in 1931.

1900–1920
Streets, Shops and Houses

HUGE WAVES BATTERING the sea front at Caroline Place. This was taken before the sea front was widened in 1910, the view being taken from a house on the corner of Pelham Street. It gives us a vivid explanation for the frequent flooding of these early nineteenth-century lodging houses. (F.S. Mann.)

THE TOWN CENTRE of 1910 with its memorial clock was alive with a variety of shops. Here, you could buy anything from a straw hat to a piano, yet the atmosphere seems uncrowded, despite the motor cycle which looks like overtaking the motor bus.

QUEEN'S ROAD in 1905. The iron railings of the cricket ground (behind the tram) were later pulled down to make way for the Queen's Parade row of shops. These are now due to be pulled down when the new town centre shopping precinct is built on the ground, regarded by so many as sacred.

ST ANDREW'S CHURCH, 1905, showing Robert Tressell's mural decoration of the chancel. This poor picture gives no idea of the dazzling colour and complexity of Tressell's work as a decorator, but one of the panels is now in the Old Town Museum. Tressell wrote the classic novel *The Ragged Trousered Philanthropists*, published in 1914.

A MOTOR BUS picking up at Wellington Place opposite the memorial clock tower. 1903.

A HORSE BUS decorated for an Edwardian carnival. It is parked at the beginning of St Helen's Road at the junction with Elphinstone Road.

THE PARADE opposite Pelham Crescent, showing on the left, the 'Hippodrome' built as a music hall in 1900. It later became the Cinema de Luxe. (Broderick.)

THE SEA FRONT opposite the Queen's Hotel. Although the sun is out, bad weather is expected: bathing-machines and boats have been pulled up out of harm's way. (Broderick.)

A MUCH PHOTOGRAPHED EDWARDIAN SCENE. Pelham Crescent with the Church of St Mary-in-the-Castle (1828) as its centre-piece. The tired-looking coachman has covered his horse with a striped blanket on what appears to be a sunny day.

CARLISLE VILLAS. You could almost step straight into the sea from these boarding houses in front of Denmark Place.

TAKEN SHORTLY BEFORE the Parade was extended in 1910. (Broderick.)

A CLOSER VIEW of the 'Hippodrome'! The façade has red terracotta tiles. It was said to be the first theatre in the country to cantilever the balcony so there were no pillars to block the view of the audience. The stage remained in place until it was converted from a cinema to a bingo hall in the 1960s. To the despair of local drama lovers, the original scenery, still *in situ*, was destroyed. (Broderick.)

MR ALAN MAXWELL, when taking over Salmon's fancy goods shop in 1969, found a dusty pile of quarter-plates in a cupboard. These turned out to be the 1900 original negatives of the fine postcard photographer F.N. Broderick. By reproducing the entire plates (to include

some of his cropping to the postcard ratio), we can see details unrevealed for over 80 years.
The Queen's Hotel, 1905.

THE BIG PLEASURE BOATS on the beach at Denmark Place. This is almost opposite the modern Homedene block of flats. (Broderick.)

AGAIN OPPOSITE PELHAM CRESCENT, this looks towards Caroline Place and Pelham Street (extreme left behind the two ladies in white). Breeds Place is on the right (behind the long seats). The shop blinds are over the windows of Mastin's the drapers. (Broderick.)

THIS FINE BURTON TERRACE was destroyed in 1937 to build the Marine Court block of flats. Burton worked with Nash and you can see the similarity here to the work of Nash in the Regent's Park area of London. (Broderick.)

ST LEONARDS PARISH CHURCH. Burton wanted to build it on the cliff behind, but his friends objected to the climb. So he had the cliff cut back and put the church at the base. A flying bomb, coming in low from over the sea, destroyed the church with freakish accuracy in 1944. (Broderick.)

LONDON ROAD from the corner of upper Norman Road. The boy on the left in his Norfolk jacket was cut from the published postcard. (Broderick.)

THE FIRST MOTOR BUS IN HASTINGS (1903) is picking up passengers from outside the Royal Victoria Hotel. The isolated figure standing at the back of the bus is mysteriously positioned. Is he looking at something which has also caught the eye of the gentleman at the rear of the top deck?

BOHEMIA ROAD opposite Tower Road, with the Bohemia Place Post Office on the left. Taken at around the time when tramlines were laid in 1905. (Broderick.)

WHO WOULD RECOGNIZE THIS PLACID SCENE as the modern nightmare of converging traffic, nervous learner drivers and alarmed pedestrians? This is where the road to Battle (left) is crossed by the modern A21 (straight ahead). Silverhill Junction, as it is still known, takes its name from an eighteenth-century farm. (Broderick.)

THIS QUIET ROAD, Chapel Park Road, is characteristic of the peace and quiet of St Leonards which attracted so many residents. At the top is St Peter's Church (built 1885), and beyond it, the shopping centre in the area known as Bohemia. (Broderick.)

CHARLES ROAD with some strange conveyances in transit. This pleasant residential terrace is opposite Gensing Gardens in St Leonards and is part of a favourite district, being built-up in the 1880s. (Broderick.)

GRAND PARADE in the 1900s. It was built independently in 1831 by some of James Burton's skilled workmen. It was formerly called Adelaide Place because Queen Adelaide spent the winter of 1837 at No. 23.

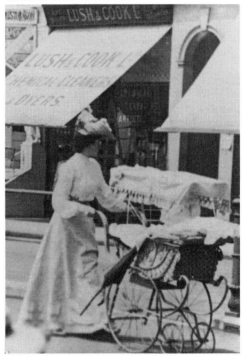

AIRING THE BABY in a grand wicker carriage at Grand Parade in the 1900s. A detail enlarged from the previous photograph.

LOWER NORMAN ROAD, St Leonards. Improvements in 'instantaneous photography' had by this time enabled the capture of movement without too much blurring. The policeman is in mid-stride, but at the price of looking ungainly. The two ladies on the left look more 'posed'

in the old manner and probably were. Bostock's shoe shop behind them dates the picture: it became Russell and Bromley's in 1907. (Broderick.)

UPPER NORMAN ROAD in the 1900s, looking eastwards to Warrior Square. The unknown, but clever photographer has captured everyone's attention and given the impression of a very lively street scene. All the people are standing still quite naturally.

LOOKING UP NORMAN ROAD towards the Methodist Church on the right. The previous picture was taken from the top of this hill looking down. (Broderick.)

BRODERICK'S VIEW of the parade, Eversfield Place (1905). The child in the perambulator nearest the camera seems remarkably large!

ANOTHER PHOTOGRAPH BY BRODERICK, this time a plain statement (i.e., a general view) of the sea front in 1905. Although having less 'human interest' than the previous photograph, this shows the photographer's enterprise. Where did he take it from? From a ladder at one of the street-lamps?

A FAMILIAR VIEW UNTIL RECENTLY. The smaller church spire was the green spire of the London Road Congregational. It was damaged in the 1987 hurricane and later demolished. The big spire is Christ Church, consecrated in 1885, which replaced the earlier church built in 1860. The Parish Hall (extreme left) is a remnant of the earlier church.

ST LEONARDS BAPTIST CHURCH. A daughter church of Wellington Square Baptist Church, it was completed in 1883. (Broderick.)

EVERYONE IS STRIDING OUT very purposefully in this Edwardian shot of Lower Maze Hill, yet it is a very hot day. (A lot of windows are open.) There was no attempt at getting anyone to pose. (Broderick.)

THE IMPOSING BURTON GATEWAY to St Leonards Gardens at the bottom of Lower Maze Hill. The huge black shadow falling just behind the two ladies is of the Assembly Rooms (now the Masonic Hall). The two ladies 'make' the picture, yet a lesser photographer than Broderick would have waited for an empty scene.

A VERY FORMAL PICTURE of Wellington Square. The garden railings went for scrap metal in the Second World War. The Castle Hotel (left) was replaced by a supermarket in 1966. It was an attractive Regency building dating from 1817.

53   HASTINGS. — Robertson Street. — LL.

LOOKING DOWN ROBERTSON STREET from White Rock in the early 1900s, we can see a motor bus at the stop by Holy Trinity Church. The nicely decorative gas-lamp, on the near left, marks the entrance to the Wellington Pub which you can still visit.

THE BOROUGH ENGINEER took this photograph of the sea wall in 1908 prior to the widening of the Parade. Behind it, on the Parade, is the Royal Oak Hotel. The proprietor was no doubt infuriated by the 'Temperance Refreshment Car' just in front of it.

Extension of Parade.
Caroline Place & Beach Terrace.

LOOKING FROM THE CORNER OF PELHAM STREET to the east, in 1910, this photograph shows the extent of the sea front widening. The 'Oxo' advertisement is on Beach Terrace and a favourite rendezvous ('Meet you at Oxo'). (Borough Engineer.)

WORK IN PROGRESS on the 1910 parade extension, looking westwards towards the Pier. The sea front is being completely changed at this point. Mid-centre is the site of the present-day Carlisle Public House. (Borough Engineer.)

TRAMLINES being laid in Hughenden Place at the corner with Mt Pleasant Road in 1905. The workmen have all taken a breather to keep still for the camera, but a striding pedestrian (on the right) has defeated the slow shutter speed.

LAYING THE TRAMLINES in Mt Pleasant in 1905. The corner of Calvert Road is very similar today except for the disappearance of the gas-lamp.

QUEEN'S ROAD, with the No. 27 tram to Hollington near St Andrew's church. When the church was demolished in 1971 the chancel murals painted by Robert Tressell were found, whitewashed over.

THIS POWER-STATION for the trams was completed in 1905. It housed six engines (3,150 hp) and had substations at Silverhill and Bulverhythe. The tramways gave work to many people. The 15 miles of track had to be cleaned and inspected every day with repair work taking place at night. The unmade road on the left is the modern Parker Road. Halfway up on the left of it, is a thatched barn. Girls are blackberrying in the hollow to the right.

THIS ADVERTISEMENT painted on a wall next to St Clement's Church had a theatrical style. Could it have been painted by one of the scene painters from one of the local theatres? The wall itself belonged to Shipman's the Chemists (in High Street, around 1898 to 1948). Several spaces are vacant, but the effect must have been startingly colourful in juxtaposition with the church. Although working in black and white, a good photographer could not have resisted the sight, but it may be a trade photograph to encourage clients.

A VERY RUSTIC VIEW of Old London Road in 1870. Tor Field is to the left, known for its allotments in after years. On the right is the pound where stray animals were held. How casually the carter is able to block this now busy road to have his picture taken!

AT THIS NOW VERY BUSY JUNCTION at the bottom of Old London Road and Harold Road, there was so little traffic that you could stand in the road to wait for the tram. 1905

BATTLE ROAD, ST LEONARDS, in 1905. The tramlines have just been laid – a portent of the future development of this village of Hollington. It was incorporated with Hastings in 1897 but in 1905 still had a separate existence.

THE GRACIOUS white, wooden swan boats were much loved by small children. This is in around 1910, but they were still to be seen on the same lake in the 30s.

VICTORIA AVENUE in the early 1900s. (Broderick.)

WALKING UP THE FAIRLIGHT ROAD in the early 1900s. Tile Kiln Farm is at the bottom of the hill on the left. (Broderick.)

THOMAS SPALDING, an elderly and prosperous paper merchant, built this pleasant Victorian villa in 1863, after pulling down the old manor house of Ore Place.

SPALDING'S VILLA (see above) was incorporated into this hugely stern building, which the Society of African Fathers, a Jesuit order, built in 1905. It subsequently housed the Army Records Office for many years but was demolished in 1987 to make way for a beautifully sited housing estate.

THE GATEWAY AND LODGE to Coghurst Hall on The Ridge. It faced the entrance to Victoria Avenue which the dark lady is just entering. Coghurst Hall belonged to the Brisco family and was designed in 1834 by Decimus Burton and demolished in 1952.

CAN YOU RECOGNIZE THIS, as the busy junction of today? The Fairlight Sanatorium (now Barrington House) is on the left. The Rye Road (1926) cuts through the centre here. The old main road (the Winchelsea Road that led to Rye) is further to the left of the picture. (Broderick.)

Mr Freeman Thomas
Liberal Candidate for Hastings

THIS ELEGANT GENTLEMAN is Freeman Freeman Thomas, the last Liberal MP for Hastings (1900–1906). As Lord Willingdon, he became Governor General of Canada (1926–1931) and Viceroy of India (1931–1936). He died in 1941.

HARVEY DU CROS, the Conservative who defeated Freeman Freeman Thomas and became MP in 1906. This witty Irishman, with the amazing whiskers, could easily be persuaded to sing 'The Wearing of the Green' at his meetings. He made his money from Dunlop tyres.

103

HARVEY DU CROS resigned as MP for Hastings in 1908. This is his son, Arthur, canvassing. He became the next MP.

AN EXCELLENT EXAMPLE of a trade photograph, with the family proudly posed outside the business. But why were the ladies left within? Mr H.P. Linch, the proprietor, is standing in the doorway of No. 40 Whitefriars Road in 1913.

THIS LARGE AND WELL-STOCKED GROCERY SHOP belonged to J.G. Brann. It stood (and still stands) at the top of the steps leading down to Beaconsfield Road, but today is three separate shops.

CAREFULLY COMPOSED PHOTOGRAPHS of shops and their staff are characteristic of the turn of the century. Was this perhaps the work of the beach photographers out of season?

ANOTHER CAREFULLY POSED TRADE PHOTOGRAPH. The female shop assistant has hardly been allowed into the picture by these stalwart males. Next door is Breeds' Brewery with a sandwich-board man having a chat. High Street, 1900s.

THE MAYOR, ALDERMAN MITCHELL, reading the proclamation of King George V to a packed Queen's Road.

THIS SOLEMN CIVIC GROUP on the steps of the Town Hall, are the Mayor of Hastings, Alderman William Perrins, with his deputy, Councillor Arthur Blackman (right). With them are the town crier (far right) and the mace bearers on each side. The town clerk lurks behind. Date 1919.

THE FAMOUS BREWERY of Breeds & Co. in the Old Town valley was established in 1836. This is the staff cricket team in 1905.

ROLLER-SKATING on St Leonards Pier in 1910. It was said that it was 'like roller-skating in a thick cloud of dust to the roar of Niagara Falls'.

ORE VILLAGE FÊTE (around 1900) in Godden's Field, Rock Lane. On the skyline, to the right of the swings, is a faint impression of the White Mill. Today, its sails are missing.

THE LORD WARDEN OF THE CINQUE PORTS, Earl Brassey, visits Priory Road Boys' School (now the Hastings Teacher Centre). The occasion was the presentation of an Australian flag on 30 September 1911.

LORD BRASSEY'S 500-ton steam yacht *The Sunbeam*, anchored off Hastings in 1911. The ship was opened to the public, rather as historic houses are today, with members of the public being rowed out to it at a shilling per head. A model is still to be seen in Hastings Museum, and Lady Brassey's book *Around the World in the Yacht Sunbeam* (still in print) gives details of the 1876–77 cruises.

THIS STAGE COACH (a private drag) has a coat of arms, but has obviously come down in the world and is being used for hiring out. The conveyance to the left is a Rolli cart. These vehicles are outside The Golden Cross in Havelock Road.

SKINNER'S MOTOR COACH to the Derby, 1911, organized by Mr Bert Sharp.

MASTIN'S THE DRAPERS' Christmas outing, January 1911. The motor coach is parked at the steep end of Wellington Square. Mastin's opened in 1872 and closed down in 1969. New shops now occupy the site in Breeds Place, just around the corner.

'PHILPOT'S XMAS CHOIR' was drawn from the staff of Philpot's the Drapers, opened as a 'lace and cap' shop in 1836. It remained trading at Nos. 37–38 Marina, St Leonards, until it closed (to a chorus of nostalgic regret) in 1986.

QUEUING AT THE GAIETY THEATRE (built 1882) in Queen's Road in around 1910. Folk in carriages are also arriving. Most of the famous players of the day appeared on this stage. The last stage show was a performance of *The Desert Song* by the Hastleons in 1932. It then continued as a cinema to the present day.

THE TWENTY FIVE STAGE-HANDS AND OTHER STAFF of the Gaiety Theatre posing in front of the splendid motor coach before their annual outing. Why are there no ladies?

THIS IS THE PROCESSION ENTRY for the 'Pageant of Heroes' week in June, 1914. Some of the 'soldiers' appear to be ladies, but they and the two smart officers are gasworks employees. The impressive figure on the right represents Sir John Moore, the hero of Corunna who had lived in Hastings.

ANOTHER GASWORKS ENTRY for the pageant. It is uncertain who the hero is in this photograph. The gasworks in the background of both photographs has now gone and the site is occupied by Safeways Supermarket.

THE CRICKET GROUND (around 1899). A parade of volunteer soldiers for the Boer War is on the far side.

THE CRICKET GROUND RESEMBLING A LAKE after heavy rain. Before drainage improvement, this and other areas of the low-lying Priory Valley were often flooded. (This is the proposed site of the new Hastings shopping centre.)

MARATHONS ARE NOT NEW! Hastings MP, Arthur Du Cros, fires the starting gun. The scene is the cricket ground, with the Town Hall and Station Road behind, 1908.

BUILDING WORKERS 1908. These are characteristic of the workmen that Robert Tressell worked with, and wrote about, in *The Ragged Trousered Philanthropists*.

THE EMPIRE DAY PARADE of police in Queen's Road, passing St Andrew's Church, 1907.

EMPIRE DAY PARADE, 24 May 1907. Originally Queen Victoria's birthday and a school holiday, after the Boer War it became Empire Day and is now Commonwealth Day. This is the Firemen's Parade.

BEACH PHOTOGRAPHER, A.M. BREACH, took this dignified party opposite White Rock. The building marked 'Kodak' is still a photographer's shop, Marriot's, opened in 1910, but the beach is no longer at road level.

A MIXED AND MORE INFORMAL GROUP, which the same photographer has shepherded together. It is worth studying the faces in detail. Some express unwilling participation. The crudely chalked code number (37A) was Mr Breach's order system.

MRS MITCHELL, described as the 'oldest flower seller in Hastings', in Robertson Street in 1904. Behind her left shoulder: a postman arrested by the sight of the camera.

THE GIRL ON THE LEFT is carrying a caged bird (probably a budgie) to use for fortune-telling. Around 1900.

THE CRICKET GROUND was used for many other sports. Behind, to the left, is the Cricketer's public house. To the extreme right are the houses that are now the site of Marks and Spencer's. To the left is The Bedford, a pub destroyed in Second World War bombing.

COMING BACK FROM THE SOUP-KITCHEN down St George's Road. Robert Tressell was already at work on his classic novel, a social indictment of such scenes in Hastings.

POOR FAMILIES CARRYING PATHETIC RECEPTACLES and queuing up at the soup kitchen on the West Hill in 1909.

A RATHER SAD PICTURE of a male flower seller at the town centre in the 1900s. Some of the poorer street traders always look a little surprised at being thought worthy enough to photograph.

THIS LEMONADE SELLER in the 1900s was either too self-conscious to look at the camera or was deliberately posed in this 'artistic' way.

ANOTHER PHOTOGRAPH difficult to date, because so many 'historic' items, from the gas-lamps to the type of camera and plate size, stayed in use for many long years. This picture was taken towards the bottom of London Road, just above Norman Road, and shows the Salvation Army with some very stoutly made music stands. Probably 1910.

THE SALVATION ARMY ('The Sally Army') at Silverhill in 1910. They are collecting 'jam jars, rags, bones etc., – in aid of the self denial fund'. The Hastings branch of the Salvation Army was founded in 1870.

OLD TOWN BOYS drinking at the fountain in front of the 'Rotunda' fish market at the bottom of High Street. The fish market was built in 1870 and demolished in 1928.

THE MAGPIES CONCERT PARTY, 1916, founded by the composer Florence Aylward (Mrs Kinder) to raise money to help the soldiers. Back row, first left: Tom Coussens, manager of Barclays Bank, St Leonards. Front row, second left: Florence Aylward; third left: Gladys Watson.

THE WINTER ORCHESTRA was one of the great success stories of Hastings. Enough money was made at summer band concerts to fund it. Here they are in 1921 on Hastings Pier. Later, they moved into the newly-built White Rock Pavilion in 1927 and became the Municipal Orchestra. (Warchawski.)

STREET MUSICIANS outside the Royal Oak public house in Caroline Place (now gone). This row of houses was between Pelham Street (Woolworth's end) and the present-day fountain at Breeds Place. The blind pianist was a well-known local entertainer in his day.

A TOUCHING PICTURE — an accordion player with his tin mug trying to earn a living on the sea front around 1910. Was his audience of one person genuinely interested, or was he merely posed?

A CAREFULLY POSED STUDY of a fisherman mending his nets. Behind the net huts is the Cliff Railway, always known to the locals as the East Hill Lift. (L.L.)

AN ENTRANCING FEATURE OF THE EDWARDIAN ERA in Hastings was the survival (from before the turn of the century) of the elegant pleasure yachts. These used to work from off the beach near the Queen's Hotel. This picture of 1905 shows the *Skylark* being put to sea. It was broken up in 1907, but yachts of this kind were to be enjoyed well into the twenties. (Broderick.)

MIXED BATHING was finally allowed in 1903. There was suddenly so great an increase in the number of bathers that these continental type cabins (seen here at the water's edge) had to be produced to meet the demand. Before this time, mixed bathers had to keep 100 yards apart.

THE OLD-FASHIONED BATHING-HUTS had enormous wheels so that you could step straight into the sea when they were pushed forward.

A PEACEFUL AND ALMOST DREAM-LIKE VIEW of Caroline Place. It was named after Queen Caroline, the rejected wife of George IV. Although she never visited Hastings, the inhabitants were stubbornly loyal to her, perhaps because her husband favoured Brighton.

THE WHITE ROCK BATHS (opened 1874) with the beautiful bandstand. When the baths were built, the sea front was only 10 ft wide and the roof of the baths formed the parade extension. (Broderick.)

A Happy New Year.

31 HASTINGS. — The East Parade. — LL.

THE POSTCARDS taken by the French photographer, 'L.L.' (Louis Levy), have a different 'feel' to those of the very English Broderick. The policeman by the railing stands in a pose reminiscent of a French gendarme as he gazes at a nervous small boy.

16 HASTINGS. — The Parade. — LL.

WHITE ROCK — with a French photographer's eye for the rear view of shapely ladies. He makes one of them the centre-piece and achieves an almost Parisian effect. This was at a date when Edward VII was actively encouraging Anglo-French relations. The 'Souvenir Normand', strengthening ties with Normandy, was very active in Hastings and Battle.

THE PUFF OF SMOKE to the left of the picture shows the presence of a corporation steamroller. This corner of Denmark Place opposite the Queen's Hotel was destroyed by a German bomb in the Second World War. It is now Homedene House.

THE BOVRIL ADVERTISEMENT is on Carlisle Villas in front of the Carlisle Hotel. To the left is the rump of the horse used to draw up the boats.

APART FROM DRAMATICALLY HIGH SEAS, postcard photographers found views of wet weather to be unsaleable. This unknown postcard photographer has, however, been unable to resist the wet reflections and so made this truthful statement about typical summer weather. Around 1900.

ALTHOUGH INDISTINCT, this Edwardian postcard has some interesting features: the lady approaching us is wiping her eye, the sandwich-board man is old and lame (he has a stick) and the rowing boats have been firmly tied to the upturned boats covering them. The Boer War Memorial was built of red Peterhead granite (1903) with flags of gun-metal.

A SCORCHING DAY. Blinds are out at the hotels along Robertson Terrace. In the centre is the Albany Hotel, destined to be destroyed in a 1943 air raid. Many troops stationed in Hastings were killed there. It is now rebuilt as Albany Court flats.

BELOW THE OUTLINE OF THE PIER is the notorious outfall (still to be seen today) of the polluted Priory Stream. It rises at the top of Alexandra Park and was culverted when town development began. Taken in the 1900s.

SAND-CASTLE COMPETITIONS were held on the beach at low tide. Here, an elaborate sand-house appears to be the centre of attention. To the middle-left, above the crowded Parade, is the white sandstone rock, which gives this part of the sea front its name, White Rock.

CHILDREN wearing bonnets and Edwardian ladies of the early 1900s protecting their complexions with umbrellas. Today we realize how sensible they were.

THE CHILDREN ARE STANDING BESIDE A ROPE used for hauling off the boats. A large anchor was permanently buried in the sand and used to give the necessary purchase. Today, these anchors can still be found in the sand at low tide. Taken in the 1900s.

EVERSFIELD PLACE, 1905. The prosperous family of four with the jaunty little girl are passing a tram-stop. The wife has lowered her head at the sight of the camera. (Broderick.)

A MORE MODERN VIEW (1930s) of the Upper Parade at Eversfield Place. Compare it with the Broderick photograph above. The reconstructed parade was designed to create the atmosphere of a ship's deck.

IT HAD ALWAYS BEEN DIFFICULT to drag the heavy bathing-machines out of the water in rough weather. Bathing-cabins (a continental idea) were introduced in 1906 and soon replaced the old machines, but here the old and the new are side by side at St Leonards Pier.

A SOMBRE VIEW of St Leonards pier from the west. A funeral procession is entering St Leonards Parish Church. This is a colour tinted postcard of a type then beginning to be printed in Saxony, Germany.

PASSENGERS ARE LEAVING the steamer *Halcyon* at Hastings Pier in 1905. This was one of the finest steamers visiting Hastings.

A COLOUR TINTED POSTCARD printed in Germany shows this paddle-steamer beside the eastern style pier pavilion. Steamers first began to use Hastings Pier in 1885. (This fanciful 'eastern' pavilion was burnt down in 1917.)

THE SEAGULL, an iron paddle-steamer of 107 tons, plying from Hastings Pier. Built in 1877, she was bought in 1891 by the Hastings and St Leonards Steamship Co. and was registered in the name of F.J. Parsons, publisher of the local paper, the *Hastings and St Leonards Observer*. She was sold to be broken up after only three years service.

IT IS DIFFICULT TO DATE THIS PHOTOGRAPH, because it is one of the most photographed views of the fishing beach, and these fishing boats have been the same for decades. Only in recent years have they begun to lose their uniform black hulls and have different colours. This could be 1900.

1912.

Photo. by The Rev. A. Cyril Pears

A STRIKING AMATEUR PHOTOGRAPH of the Dutch East Indiaman The *Amsterdam* in 1912. Lost in the sand of Bulverhythe in 1749, its timbers can still be seen at low tide. Artefacts from the wreck can be seen in the Shipwreck Heritage Museum at Rock-a-Nore.

HASTINGS AWOKE one morning in 1919 to find this huge German submarine (the U118) on the beach opposite Denmark Place. Some of the astonished locals have stretched themselves out on the shingle to gaze at prolonged leisure. The mystery was soon explained. The submarine had been allocated to France as one of the spoils of the First World War. On tow to Cherbourg, the tow-rope snapped and the submarine was washed ashore. She was later broken up and removed, except for the keel. This forgotten keel was uncovered by the tide in the 1950s and the last vestige of a big talking point was then finally disposed of.

A MORE DETAILED VIEW of the submarine's superstructure, with a totally unconcerned child kneeling and playing almost in its shadow.

AN AMATEUR PHOTOGRAPH of Lord Brassey's yacht, *The Sunbeam*. He converted her into a hospital ship in the First World War.

SECTION THREE

Between the Wars

ALTHOUGH THIS IS WHITE ROCK in the 1920s and the fashions have changed so obviously, this scene would have been recognizable to the Edwardians and late Victorians. The same type of striped beach-hut lines the sea wall for discreet undressing. At this date, the indoor White Rock Baths were almost derelict. They were being taken over for remodelling by the corporation for who wished to 'pep up' the amenities. The baths opened in 1930 with two splendid swimming baths, a Turkish bath and 16 kinds of medicinal bath (including the virtues of Hastings seaweed).

A FAVOURITE VIEW OF HASTINGS and St Leonards looking west. Hastings Pier, with St Leonards pier beyond, in the 1930s.

VIEWS WITHOUT PEOPLE are often boring, but this view of the cricket ground (looking north-east towards South Terrace) repays close inspection. It shows the gasholders (now demolished) behind the terrace at the left-hand end and the spire of St Andrew's Church (also now demolished) at the other. At each end of the terrace itself is a public house; the Princes Pub (left) and The Cricketers (right), both have survived. The Cricketers is famous for having been patronized by the author, Robert Tressell. Between the two is the Unitarian Church and the Friends' Meeting House.

DESPITE THE OLD MOTOR CARS, this is a difficult photograph to date. It shows the north side of Wellington Square. The three-storey house in the distant corner (behind the street-lamp) was not part of the original square and no longer exists.

WELLINGTON SQUARE in the 1930s. The Glenroyde Hotel on the corner is now converted into flats. Next door (up the steps on the raised level) is Wellington College, a school for young ladies where Victorian manners were still being taught. These young ladies used to wave to the office-boys in the *Evening Argus* office (extreme right), visible to them from the school's back windows.

BREEDS PLACE in the 1930s. James Lansdell built this Regency style terrace in 1829.

THIS CAFÉ IN WELLINGTON PLACE was one of the most popular in Hastings. Who among older residents cannot remember its penny ice-cream cornets? It was founded by Lorenzo Dimarco (left) in 1905 and was finally closed by the family in 1985.

PELHAM CRESCENT in the 1930s with rock-gardens and shelters as a feature of the reconstructed sea front.

THE FINE IONIC PORTICO of St Mary's-in-the-Castle. A long-term conservation project is under way on this Regency Church — an outstanding contribution to architectural values by the Borough of Hastings.

THE EARLY MORNING SUNLIGHT is shining upon the eighteenth-century brass chandeliers in St Clement's Church. The colours on the pillars, and the poster on the wall indicate that a commemorative service has taken place. Perhaps it is just after the Armistice in 1918, but this attractive photograph is undated and unsigned. The east window was destroyed by bombing, and the new window was designed by Philip Cole, a former principal of the Hastings School of Art.

A SCENE many local people will remember: High Street in the 1930s. The Swan Hotel was destroyed in a 1943 German air raid. Many people were killed and the site is now a memorial garden. Also destroyed were the timber-framed houses opposite the old Town Hall clock.

THE HOME OF THE RICHEST MAN in Hastings in the eighteenth century, John Collier, the Hastings agent for the Duke of Newcastle. His stables (almost opposite this house and behind the photographer) are today the Stables Theatre.

CARLISLE PARADE with the underground car park in the course of construction in 1931. With government help, this scheme provided work for many people without jobs.

THE COMPLETED UNDERGROUND CAR PARK was considered very advanced in 1931.

10. Eversfield Place and New Covered Parade, Hastings.

THIS NEW 'COVERED PARADE' of the 1930s was instantly dubbed 'bottle alley' by the natives because of its unique decor – mosaics made from broken glass from the town's rubbish tip. This early example of conservation and recycled material deserves to be remembered.

THIS OLYMPIC STANDARD SWIMMING-POOL was opened in 1933 and designed by the so-called 'Concrete King' of Hastings, Sidney Little. A forceful character, he was the Borough Engineer who rebuilt the sea front. This particular example of his massive self-confidence cost £60,000.

A SUNNY WINTER DAY in the late 1930s. Walkers are enjoying the newly-built Lower Parade at St Leonards. The 'sun-trap' shelters were very popular. The big new building mid-centre is Marine Court, built to resemble the superstructure of a passenger liner. It housed 153 flats and 3 restaurants.

THE NEWLY OPENED SUN LOUNGE (part of the 1930s development) with St Leonards Pier in the background. This pier was cut in half as a precaution against invasion at the beginning of the Second World War. Its last rusty remains were removed in 1951.

OUTSIDE PARK ROAD CHURCH, Upper Park Road, in 1930. The Victorian looking mayor was in normal formal dress for inspecting the Boys' Brigade. He is Councillor George Holt Ormerod, a highly successful mayor and a very lively and handsome old chap. Behind him (in the peaked cap and clearly dwarfed by the great man) is Captain G. Dubois. At least one of the boys looks about to burst.

BIDDY STONHAM. FAMOUS TUB MAN
Greetings From Hastings

A POPULAR POSTCARD of Biddy Stonham, the Hastings tubman. A superb seaside entertainer, he would engagingly shout: 'Would any lady like to come in the tub?' Any lady foolhardy enough to do so would be spun round and round until Biddy himself fell off and the lady fell out.

BIDDY STONHAM, the tubman, with his entourage of assistants. One is wheeling the famous barrel and the other bears his paddles. Biddy sports flowers in his hat and disdains footwear. The date is 1924.

A TRULY ENGLISH SCENE. Local umpire Barry Funnell confers with the famous test match umpire Frank Chester and groundsman Alfred Dengate in 1940.

ACKNOWLEDGEMENTS

East Sussex County Library, Hastings. Hastings Museum and Art Gallery for permission to copy photographs from their collections. Victoria Williams, Curator, Hastings Museum and Brion Purdey, Principal Librarian, Hastings & Rother Area for their much appreciated help and advice. David Padgham, for the loan of pictures from his own collection and help with identification. Simon Gooch, of Marriotts Photo Stores for his technical advice. David Vivian Haines, for all his help.